# Shall I Go To God?

## Horatius Bonar

**BAKER BOOK HOUSE**
Grand Rapids, Michigan

Paperback edition issued 1977
by Baker Book House Company
ISBN: 0-8010-0713-5

PHOTOLITHOPRINTED BY CUSHING - MALLOY, INC.
ANN ARBOR, MICHIGAN, UNITED STATES OF AMERICA
1977

# CONTENTS

# HOW SHALL I GO TO GOD?

—o—

IT is with our *sins* that we go to
God, for we have nothing else to go
with that we can call our own. This
is one of the lessons that we are so
slow to learn; yet without learning
this we cannot take one right step
in that which we call a religious life.

To look up some good thing in our
past life, or to get up some good thing
now, if we find that our past does not
contain any such thing, is our first
thought when we begin to inquire
after God, that we may get the great
question settled between Him and us,
as to the forgiveness of our sins.

"In His favor is life;" and to be without this favor is to be unhappy here, and to be shut out from joy hereafter. There is no life worthy of the name of life save that which flows from His assured friendship. Without that friendship, our life here is a burden and a weariness; but with that friendship we fear no evil, and all sorrow is turned into joy.

"How shall I be happy?" was the question of a weary soul who had tried a hundred different ways of happiness, and had always failed.

"Secure the favor of God," was the prompt answer, by one who had himself tasted that the "Lord is gracious."

"Is there no other way of being happy?"

"None, none," was the quick and

decided reply. " Man has been trying other ways for six thousand years, and has utterly failed, and are *you* likely to succeed ? "

" No, not likely; and I don't want to go on trying. But this favor of God seems such a shadowy thing, and God Himself so far off, that I know not which way to turn."

" God's favor is no shadow; it is real beyond all other realities; and He Himself is the nearest of all near beings, as accessible as He is gracious."

" That favor of which you speak has always seemed to me a sort of *mist*, of which I can make nothing."

" Say rather it is *sunshine* which a mist is hiding from you."

" Yes, yes, I believe you; but how shall I get through the mist into the sunshine beyond ?   It seems so difficult, and to require such a length of time!"

"*You* make that distant and difficult which God has made simple and near and easy."

"Are there no difficulties, do you mean to say?"

"In one sense, a thousand; in another, none."

"How is that?"

"Did the Son of God put difficulties in the sinner's way when He said to the multitude, 'Come unto Me, and I will give you rest'?"

"Certainly not; He meant them to go at once to Him, as He stood there, and as they stood there, and He would give them rest."

"Had *you* then been upon the spot, what difficulties should you have found?"

"None, certainly; to speak of difficulty when I was standing by the side of the Son of God would have been folly, or worse."

"Did the Son of God suggest difficulty to the sinner when He sat on Jacob's well, by the side of the Samaritan? Was not all difficulty anticipated or put away by these wondrous words of Christ, 'thou wouldst have asked, and I would have given'?"

"Yes, no doubt; the asking and the giving was all. The whole transaction is finished on the spot. Time and space, distance and difficulty, have nothing to do with the matter; the giving was to follow the asking as a matter of course. So far all is plain. But I would ask: Is there no barrier here?"

"None whatever, if the Son of God really came to save the lost; if

He came for those who were only partly lost, or who could partly save themselves, the barrier is infinite. This I admit; nay, insist upon."

"Is the being lost, then, no barrier to our being saved?"

"Foolish question, which may be met by a foolish answer. Is your being thirsty a hindrance to your getting water or is being poor a hindrance to your obtaining riches as a gift from a friend?"

"True; it is my thirst that fits me for the water and my poverty that fits me for the gold."

"Ah, yes, the Son of Man came not to call the righteous but sinners to repentance. If you be not wholly a sinner, there is a barrier; if you be wholly such, there is none!"

"Wholly a sinner! Is that really my character?"

"No doubt of that. If you doubt it, go and search your Bible. God's testimony is that you are wholly a sinner, and must deal with Him as such, for the whole need not a physician, but they that are sick."

"Wholly a sinner, well!—but must I not get quit of some of my sins before I can expect blessing from Him?"

"No, indeed; He alone can deliver you from so much as even one sin; and you must go at once to Him with all that you have of evil, how much soever that may be. If you be not wholly a sinner, you don't wholly need Christ, for He is out and out a Saviour; He does not help you to save yourself, nor do you help Him to save you. He does all, or nothing. A half salvation will only do for those who are not completely lost. He ' His own self bare our sins in His own body on the tree.' " *

It was in some such way as the above that Luther found his way into the peace and liberty of Christ. The story of his deliverance is an instructive one, as showing how the stumbling-blocks of self-righteousness are removed by the full exhibition of the gospel in its freeness, as the good news of God's love to the unloving and unlovable, the good news of pardon to the sinner, without merit and without money, the good news of PEACE WITH GOD, solely through the propitiation of Him who hath made peace by the blood of His cross.

One of Luther's earliest difficulties was that he must get repentance wrought within himself; and having accomplished this, he was to carry this

* 1 Peter ii. 24.

repentance as a peace-offering or recommendation to God.   If this repentance could not be presented as a posi-
tive recommendation, at least it could
be urged as a plea in mitigation of
punishment.

"How can I dare believe in the
favor of God," he said, "so long as
there is in me no real conversion?   I
must be changed before He can receive me."

He is answered that the "conversion," or "repentance," of which he is
so desirous, can never take place so
long as he regards God as a stern
and unloving Judge.   It is the *goodness of God* that leadeth to repentance,* and without the recognition
of this "goodness" there can be no
softening of heart.   An impenitent
sinner is one who is despising the

* Romans ii. 4.

riches of His goodness and forbear-
ance and long-suffering.

Luther's aged counsellor tells him
plainly that he must be done with
penances and mortifications, and all
such self-righteous preparations for
securing or purchasing the Divine
favor.

That voice, Luther tells us touch-
ingly, seemed to come to him from
heaven: " All true repentance begins
with the knowledge of the forgiving
love of God."

As he listens light breaks in, and
an unknown joy fills him. Nothing
between him and God! Nothing between him and pardon! No preliminary goodness, or preparatory feeling!
He learns the Apostle's lesson, "Christ
died for the *ungodly;*" * God "justifieth the *ungodly*." †   All the evil that

* Romans v. 6.          † Romans iv. 5.

is in him cannot hinder this justifica-
tion; and all the goodness (if such
there be) that is in him cannot assist
in obtaining it. He must be received
as a sinner, or not at all. The pardon
that is proffered recognizes only his
*guilt;* and the salvation provided in
the cross of Christ regards him simply
as *lost.*

But the sense of guilt is too deep
to be easily quieted. Fear comes
back again, and he goes once more
to his aged adviser, crying, " Oh, my
sin, my sin!" as if the message of
forgiveness which he had so lately
received was too good news to be
true, and as if sins like his could not
be so easily and so simply forgiven.

" What! would you be only a pretended sinner, and therefore need only
a pretended Saviour?"

So spake his venerable friend, and

then added, solemnly, "Know that
Jesus Christ is the Saviour of great
and real sinners, who are deserving
of nothing but utter condemnation."

"But is not God sovereign in His
electing love?" said Luther; "perhaps
I may not be one of His chosen."

"Look to the wounds of Christ,"
was the answer, "and learn there
God's gracious mind to the children
of men.  In Christ we read the name
of God, and learn what He is, and
how He loves; the Son is the revealer
of the Father; and the Father sent
the Son to be the Saviour of the
world."

"I believe in the forgiveness of
sins," said Luther to a friend one
day, when tossing on a sick bed; "but
what is that to me?"

"Ah," said his friend, "does not
that include your own sins?  You be-

lieve in the forgiveness of DAVID's sins, and of PETER's sins, why not of your own? The forgiveness is for you as much as for DAVID or PETER."

Thus Luther found rest. The gospel, thus believed, brought liberty and peace. He knew that he was forgiven because God had said that forgiveness was the immediate and sure possession of all who believed the good news.

In the settlement of the great question between the sinner and God, there was to be no bargaining and no price of any kind. The basis of settlement was laid eighteen hundred years ago; and the mighty transaction on the cross did all that was needed as a price. "It is finished," is God's message to the sons of men in their inquiry, "What shall we do to be saved?" This *completed transaction*

supersedes all man's efforts to justify
himself, or to assist God in justifying
him. We see Christ crucified, and
God in Christ reconciling the world
unto Himself, *not imputing unto men
their trespasses;* and this non-imputa-
tion is the result solely of what was
done upon the cross, where the trans-
ference of the sinner's guilt to the
Divine surety was once and for ever
accomplished. It is of that transaction
that the gospel brings us the "good
news," and whosoever believeth it becomes partaker of all the benefits which
that transaction secured.

"But am I not to be indebted to
the Holy Spirit's work in my soul?"

"Undoubtedly; for what hope can
there be for you without the Almighty
Spirit, who quickeneth the dead?"

"If so, then ought I not to wait for
His impulses, and having got them,

may I not present the feelings which
He has wrought in me as reasons why
I should be justified?"

"No, in no wise. You are not
justified by the Spirit's work, but
by Christ's alone; nor are the mo-
tions of the Spirit in you the grounds
of your confidence, or the reasons for
your expecting pardon from the Judge
of all. The Spirit works in you, not
to prepare you for being justified, or
to make you fit for the favor of God,
but to *bring you to the cross*, just as
you are. For the cross is the only
place where God deals in mercy with
the transgressor."

It is at the cross that we meet God
in peace and receive His favor. There
we find not only the blood that washes,
but the righteousness which clothes
and beautifies, so that henceforth we
are treated by God as if our own

unrighteousness had passed away, and the righteousness of His own Son were actually ours.

This is what the apostle calls " imputed" righteousness,* or righteousness so reckoned to us by God as that we are entitled to all the blessings which that righteousness can obtain for us. Righteousness got up by ourselves, or put into us by another, we call *infused*, or *imparted*, or *inherent* righteousness; but righteousness belonging to another reckoned to us by God as if it were our own, we call *imputed* righteousness. It is of this that the apostle speaks when he says, "Put ye on the Lord Jesus Christ." † Thus Christ *represents* us: and God deals with us as represented by Him. Righteousness within will

---

* Romans iv. 6, 8, 11, 22, 24.
† Romans xiii. 14; Galatians iii. 27.

follow necessarily and inseparably; but
we are not to wait in order to get
it before going to God for the righteousness of His only begotten Son.

Imputed righteousness must come
*first*.   You cannot have the righteousness *within* till you have the righteousness *without;* and to make your
own righteousness the price which you
give to God for that of His Son, is
to dishonor Christ, and to deny His
cross.   The Spirit's work is not to
make us holy, in order that we may
be pardoned, but to show us the cross,
where the pardon is to be found by
the unholy; so that having found the
pardon there, we may begin the life
of holiness to which we are called.

That which God presents to the sinner is an *immediate pardon*, "Not by
works of righteousness which we have
done," but by the great work of right-

eousness finished for us by the Substitute.  Our qualification for obtaining that righteousness is *that we are unrighteous*, just as the sick man's qualification for the physician is *that he is sick*.

Of a previous goodness, preparatory to pardon, the gospel says nothing.  Of a preliminary state of religious feeling as a necessary introduction to the grace of God, the apostles never spoke.  Fears, troubles, self-questionings, bitter cries for mercy, forebodings of judgment, and resolutions of amendment, may, in point of time, have preceded the sinner's reception of the good news; but they did not constitute his fitness, nor make up his qualification.  He would have been quite as welcome without them.  They did not make the pardon more complete, more gracious, or more free.  The sinner's *wants* were all his arguments:—"God be merciful to me a sinner." He *needed* salvation, and he went to God for it, and got it just because he needed it, and because God delights in the poor and needy. He *needed* pardon, and he went to God for it, and obtained it without merit or money. "When he had NOTHING TO PAY, God frankly forgave." It was the having nothing to pay that drew out the frank forgiveness.

Ah, this is *grace*. "This is *love*, not that we loved God, but that He loved us!" He loved us, even when we were dead in sins. He loved us, not because we were rich in goodness, but because He was "rich in mercy"; not because we were worthy of His favor, but because He delighted in loving-kindness. His welcome to us comes from His own graciousness, not from our lovableness. "Come unto

Me, all ye that labor and are heavy laden, and I will give you rest." Christ invites the weary! It is this weariness that fits you for Him, and Him for you. Here is the *weariness*, there is the *resting-place!* They are side by side. Do you say, "That resting-place is not for me?" What! Is it not for the weary? Do you say, "But I cannot make use of it?" What! Do you mean to say, "I am so weary that I cannot sit down?" If you had said, "I am so weary that I cannot stand, nor walk, nor climb," one could understand you. But to say, "I am so weary that I cannot sit down," is simple folly, or something worse, for you are making a merit and a work of your sitting down; you seem to think that to sit down is to do some great thing which will require a long and prodigious effort.

Let us listen then to the gracious words of the Lord: "If thou knewest the gift of God, and who it is that saith to thee, Give Me to drink; thou wouldest have asked of Him, and He would have given thee living water." * Thou wouldest have asked, and He would have given! That is all. How real, how true, how free; yet how simple! Or let us listen to the voice of the servant in the person of Luther. "Oh, my dear brother, learn to know Christ and Him crucified. Learn to sing a new song; to despair of previous work, and to cry to Him, Lord Jesus, Thou art my righteousness, and I am Thy sin. Thou hast taken on Thee what was mine, and given to me what is Thine. What I was, Thou becamest, that I might be what I was not. Christ dwells only

* John iv. 10.

with sinners. Meditate often on this love of Christ, and you will taste its sweetness." Yes; pardon, peace, life, are all of them *gifts*, Divine gifts, brought down from heaven by the Son of God, presented personally to each needy sinner by the God and Father of our Lord Jesus Christ. They are not to be *bought*, but *received;* as men receive the sunshine, complete and sure and free. They are not to be earned or deserved by exertions or sufferings, or prayers or tears; but *accepted* at once as the purchase of the labors and sufferings of the great Substitute. They are not to be waited for, but *taken* on the spot without hesitation or distrust, as men take the loving gift of a generous friend. They are not to be claimed on the ground of *fitness* or *goodness*, but of *need* and *unworthiness*, of poverty and emptiness.

# WHAT IS MY HOPE?

—o—

"I HOPED by this time to have been at the top," said an old man, who had set out one pleasant autumn morning to climb the hill behind his dwelling. But he had mistaken the way, and was farther from the top than when he set out. He returned weary and disappointed. Like those of whom Job speaks, "He was confounded, *because he had hoped*" (Job vi. 20).

"I hoped by this time to have been happy," said a young man, as he sat at the helm of his splendid yacht, and steered her along in the sunshine. But with all his gold, and the pleasure

which gold buys, he was duller and
sadder than he was ten years before,
when he set out to " enjoy life." He
had mistaken the way, and his soul
was emptier than ever. He sighed
and looked round upon the blue waves
in vain; they could not help him.
" He was confounded *because he had
hoped.*" He had mistaken the way.
Year after year had passed, and he
had been going farther and farther
from happiness. God was not in all
his thoughts.

" I hoped by this time to have had
peace with God," said a man of sixty,
one Sabbath morning as he walked
to the house of God. But he seemed
as one who was farther off than ever
from peace; and the thought of ad-
vancing years, without any settlement
for eternity, made him sad. He had
mistaken the way. He had labored,

and prayed, and fasted, and done many good works; he had done all but the one thing,—he had not taken Christ. He had not counted all things but loss for Christ; he had not rested his soul on the one resting-place. His life had been a life of doing, but not of believing; of doubting, not of trusting; and "he was confounded *because he had hoped.*" He might have had Christ many years ago, but he preferred his own plan, and continued his laborious efforts to recommend himself to God by his devotions and doings. The peace he had been working for had not come; and the peace for which the Son of God had wrought, and which He had finished for the sinner, he had not accepted.

It is one thing to hope, and it is another thing to hope well and truly. To hope aright is to hope according to what God has revealed concerning our future.

Much has been written of "the pleasures of hope"; and much that is true and beautiful has been said of these "pleasures"; for they are many, and man clings to them even in days of darkness and despair. It is not a wrong thing to hope. God has put hope in every human breast; and the Book of God dwells much upon it, and upon "the things hoped for." It is "good that a man should hope," said the prophet. "Hope on, hope ever," are the expressive words of a motto which has cheered many. Hope is "the anchor of the soul," and is frequently, in pictures, and devices, and emblems, thus set forth,—an anchor firmly fixed on the solid shore, and holding fast a vessel beaten by wind and wave.

But, in order to be the anchor of the soul, hope must be something surer and better than what man usually calls by that name. For man's hopes are often but his own wishes and fancies; and even when they go beyond these, and occupy themselves with what is really true and lawful, they are not to be trusted, and they endure but for a season. They disappoint, but do not fill. They cheat and mock him who trusts them. They abide not, but depart, leaving behind them only a void and aching heart.

They fall to pieces of themselves, even when no hand touches them, and no storm crushes them. They are not to be trusted for a day. "Vanity of vanities, saith the Preacher; all is vanity."

One August evening, just before sunset, we saw a rainbow suddenly appear. It seemed to rise out of the dark clouds that hung in the sky, and drew our eyes by its completeness; for nothing seemed wanting either in color or in position, to its perfection. But if it was one of the brightest, it was also one of the briefest we had ever seen. It had scarcely taken its place on the cloud when it disappeared. That fair bow was like man's hope, as brief as it was bright, as disappointing as it was promising. It melted off the sky, though no hand touched it, and no tempest shook it, leaving nothing behind but the cheerless cloud, which it had for a few moments brightened. "What is man?" it said. What are man's hopes, and joys, and plans? They rise and fall; they come and go; they shine, and then return into darkness. "The things that are seen are temporal."

We remember one peculiar day in the desert of Sinai,—a day not exactly of rain, but of showers, with clear sunshine between. Over some high black rocks to the left of us thin mists hung, or rather rapidly passed across the brown precipices. On these, rainbow after rainbow formed itself in beautiful succession; six or seven of these suddenly shining out, and then disappearing, one after another,—the brightest yet frailest things we had ever seen; so like what is real and abiding, yet so unreal and perishable. How like they were to the dreams and hopes of man, disappointing and cheating human hearts with unsubstantial beauty! To such dreams and hopes the poor heart clings, not in youth merely, but to old age; and by means of these vain brightnesses is drawn away from Him who is brighter than all earthly

brightnesses,—the "brightness of Je-
hovah's glory and the express image
of His person; whose glory changes
not; who is the same yesterday, to-
day, and for ever."

O man, when wilt thou be wise,
and fix thine eye only on that which
endureth for ever; on that which will
fill thy heart and gladden thy soul to
all eternity?

There was an old Scottish family,
to whom belonged large estates, and
who had lived together for many years
in unbroken completeness. One evening they gathered all together, with
relatives and friends,—father, mother,
sisters, cousins, with the heir of the
estate as the centre of the happy circle. That evening was among the
last of the completeness. Within a
few years all was changed, and each
member of that circle, that had sat

in gladness round the family hearth, was gathered into the family vault. The estate passed into other hands, and the old trees waved over other heads. The hopes that shone in each face that evening were speedily crushed, and the frailty of earth's fairest faces and fondest affections was sadly shown. We never look upon that old family mansion without calling to mind some text that tells of the vanity of human expectations. In a dying world like this, we need a sure and undying hope.

It is written, "Thou destroyest the hope of man." Yes, even so. Not only does man's hope fall to pieces of itself, but God destroys it before its time. It springs up in a night, and withers in a night, because God smites it. Man cannot be trusted here with the endurance of any earthly things. They become idols, and must

be broken; for "the idols He will utterly abolish." Our cherished hopes
of a bright future here—of a long life,
of health, of comfort, of money, of
prosperity—must be checked, else we
should make earth our home and our
heaven, forgetting the glory to be
revealed, and the pleasures that are
at God's right hand for ever. "As
many as I love, I rebuke and chasten;
be zealous, therefore, and repent."

But God quenches no hope without
presenting a brighter one,—one that
will last for ever; for He does not
mock the creature that He has made,
nor wither up his fairest flowers without a reason, and that reason fraught
both with wisdom and with love. He
cares for us. He yearns over us. He
would fain make us happy. He loves
us too well to cheat us with dreams.

*Man's* hope must be destroyed, that

*God's* hope may be built upon its ruins.
The human is swept away only that
the divine may come in its stead. The
temporal is in mercy wrested from our
grasp, that the eternal may be our
portion and inheritance.

There is, then, that which God calls
"the BETTER hope,"—a hope full of
immortality; a hope which God Himself gives, and of which no man can
rob us. It is divine and everlasting.
It brings with it the peace which passeth all understanding; and it contains
in it the joy unspeakable and full of
glory. No disappointment in it, and
no mockery! It is sure and glorious,
like Him from whom it comes to us.
It is connected with a crown, with an
inheritance, with a kingdom, with a
glory which fadeth not away, with an
eternity of joy such as eye hath not
seen, nor ear heard.

The hope which God sets before
us is no doubtful thing, but sure and
glorious. It rests upon His gospel,
in believing which we become men of
hope.

For nothing save a believed gospel
can give us aught of hope,—at least
of that which God calls by that name.
A believed gospel brings us peace;
and, with the peace, it brings us hope.
The peace is sure and steadfast; so
also is the hope it brings.

This gospel is the good news concerning Him who died and was buried and rose again. The thirty-three
years between His cradle and His
cross embrace the whole compass of
the good news. The story of His
birth, and life, and death, contains all
we need to know for peace. Into the
soul of him who receives that divine
story this peace enters, and, there it

makes its abode,—peace in believing,
peace with God through our Lord
Jesus Christ. "To him that worketh
not, but believeth" (Rom. iv. 5), this
peace belongs; and he who has the
peace has the hope,—a hope that
maketh not ashamed.

Blessed union of peace and hope!
We cannot have the hope without the
peace, and we cannot have the peace
without the hope (Rom. v. 1, 2). The
belief of the good news makes us par-
takers of both.

Herein is love! For thus we see
God providing not only for our present, but for our future, setting before our
eyes a crown and kingdom, and mean-
while giving us peace with Himself
here on earth until that kingdom come.
Herein is love! For thus we see God
in His pity drying up our earthly
wells, and at the same time opening

for us the wells of salvation,—"the fountain of the water of life."

Lift up thine eyes, O man, and look unto that future which lies before you! What is it to be? Dark or bright? Your life is but a vapor. Will you not make sure of the life everlasting? It is within your reach. It is pressed upon your acceptance by Him who came to give hope to the hopeless, life to the dead, peace to the troubled, rest to the weary. That which He did in dying on the cross is that which you have to rest upon for eternity. It is a sure resting-place. You need no other. He that believeth entereth into REST!

Yes; and he that believeth enters into a new life, and begins a holy walk,—a life and a walk corresponding to the faith which realizes both the grace of the Cross and the glory of the kingdom. "If any man be in Christ, he is a new creature"; and that same Holy Spirit who drew him to the Cross, is given him that he may follow Christ, and be holy as He was holy.

# INSTEAD OF ME

—o—

Many years ago, I was walking with a friend along the pleasant banks of a Scottish river, in one of the early months of summer, when the trees had just begun to show their fresh verdure and to offer us a shade from the sun. A man in rags came up to us begging. We supplied his wants somewhat, and entered into talk with him. He could not write nor read. He knew nothing of his Bible, and seemed not to care about knowing it.

"You need to be saved, do you not?"

44

"Oh yes; I suppose I do," he said.

"But do you know the way of being saved?" we asked.

"I dare say I do," was the reply.

"How, then, do you expect this?"

"I have not been a very bad man; and am doing as many good works as I can."

"But are your good works good enough to take you to heaven?"

"I think so; and I am doing my best."

"Do you not know any good works better than your own?"

"I know about the good works of the saints; but how am I to get them?"

"Do you know of no good works better than those of the saints?"

"I don't think there can be any better."

"Are not the works of the Lord

Jesus Christ better than the works of the saints?"

"Of course they are; but of what use are they to me?"

"They may be of great use to us, if we believe what God has told us about them."

"How is that?"

"If God is willing to take these works of Christ instead of yours, would not that do?"

"Yes, that it would.  But will He?"

"Yes, He will.  For this is just what He has told us; He is willing to take all that Christ has done and suffered instead of what you could do or suffer; and to give you what Christ has deserved instead of what you have deserved."

"Is that really the case?  Is God willing to put Christ instead of me?"

"Yes, He certainly is."

" But have I no good works to do myself ? "

" Plenty; but not to buy pardon with them. You are to take what Christ did as the price to be paid for your pardon; and then, having thus got a free pardon, you will work for Him who pardons you, out of love for His love to you."

" But how can I get this ? "

" By believing the gospel, or good news, which tell you about the Lord Jesus Christ : how He lived; how He died; how He was buried; how He rose again—all for sinful men; as the Bible says, 'Through this Man is preached unto you the forgiveness of sins; and by Him all that believe are justified from all things.' "

The beggar stood and wondered. The thought that another's works would do instead of his own, and

that he might get all that this other's
works deserved, seemed to strike him.

We never met again. But the
Word seemed to tell upon him; he
seemed to take it with him as something which he had never heard before
—something which seemed almost too
good news to be true.

I have more than once spoken of
this since, in illustrating the gospel,
and it seemed to tell. The man's
wonder that another's works should
do instead of his own was in itself an
insight into the effects produced by
the gospel of Christ. "Christ for us,"
is the message which we bring; Christ
"bearing our sins in His own body
on the tree"; Christ doing what we
should have done, bearing what we
should have borne; Christ nailed to
our cross, dying our death, paying

our debt—all this to bring us to God,
and to make everlasting life ours; this
is the sure word of the gospel, which
whosoever believeth is saved, and shall
never come into condemnation.

There are few who do not know
what that word "substitute" means
when used concerning common things;
but it is well that we should see how
the right knowledge of this word is
the key to the right understanding of
the gospel. "Christ for us," or Christ
our Substitute, is the gospel or glad
tidings of great joy which apostles
preached, and which we can tell, even
in these later days, to the sons of
men as their true hope. The good
news which we bring is not of what
we are commanded to do in order
that God may be reconciled to us,
but of what the Son of God has done
instead of us. He took our place

here, on earth, that we might obtain
His place in heaven. As the Perfect
One, in life and in death, as the Doer
and the Sufferer, He is presented to
us that we may get the complete ben-
efit of that perfection so soon as we
receive His gospel. All our imper-
fection, however great, is lost in the
completeness of His perfection, so that
God sees us not as we are, but as
He is. All that we are, and have
done, and have been, is lost sight of
in what He is, and has done, and has
been. "He who knew no sin was
made sin for us, that we might be
made the righteousness of God in
Him."

It is this sin-bearing completeness
of the Son of God, as the Substitute,
that the sinner rests upon. It is on
this that we take our stand in our
dealings with God. We need a sin-

bearer; and God has given us One who is altogether perfect and Divine. "The chastisement of our peace was upon Him, and with His stripes we are healed." "He, His own Self, bare our sins in His own body on the tree."

We once dealt with a young man as to this. He sat, with his Bible before him, pondering the way of life, and asking, What must I do to be saved? He was in darkness, and saw no light. He was a sinner—how was he to be saved? He was guilty—how was he to be forgiven?

"Not by works of righteousness which we have done."

"No, certainly; but how then?"

"By Christ doing the whole."

"But is this possible? Can I be saved by another doing the whole for me?"

"It is not only possible, but it is certain. This is the way; the only way. It is God's one way of saving the sinner."

"And have I nothing to do?"

"Nothing in order to be saved."

"But tell me how this is to be."

"Let us come back to the truth about the Substitute. You know what that is?"

"I do. But how does this bear upon my case?"

"Christ offers Himself to you as your Substitute; to do what you should have done, to suffer what you should have suffered, to pay what you should have paid."

"Do you mean that Christ has actually paid my debt, and that this is what I am to believe in order to be saved?"

"No. Your debt is not paid till you believe: then it is paid—paid once for all, once and for ever; but not till then."

"How, then, is the work of Christ, as the Substitute, good news to me?"

"There is enough of money lodged in the bank to pay all your debts twice over; and you have only to apply for it. Hand in your check, and you will get the money at once."

"I see; I see. It is 'believing' that brings me into actual possession of all the fruits of the sin-bearing work upon the cross."

"Yes; just so. Or, let me put it in another way. Christ died for our sins. He is the Substitute. He is presented to you as such. Are you willing to take Him as such, that He may pay all your debts and forgive all your sins?"

"Yes. But let me see this more fully; for it seems too simple."

"Well; put it thus: God has provided a Substitute for the guilty, who, eighteen hundred years ago, suffered for sins, the Just for the unjust. The Father presents that complete Substitute to you, and asks your consent to the exchange. The Son presents Himself to you, offering to be your Substitute. The Holy Spirit presents Him to you as a Substitute. Do you consent? The Father is willing, the Son is willing, the Spirit is willing. Are you willing? Do you give your consent?"

"Is that it?" said he.

"It is. Your consenting to take Christ as your Substitute is faith."

"Is that it?" said he again. And the light broke upon him. "Christ our Substitute was the dawning of the day."

Thus it is that the sinner's chain

is broken, and he is set free to serve
God.   First liberty, then service; the
service of men set free from condemnation and from bondage.   It is in accepting the Divine Substitute that the
sinner is set free to serve the living
God.   The liberty flowing from forgiveness, thus received, is the true beginning of a holy life.

If, then, I am to live a holy life, I
must begin with the Substitute.   I
must deal with Him for pardon and
deliverance.   Thus being by Him " delivered out of the hands of our enemies, we serve God without fear, in
holiness and righteousness all the days
of our life."

If I am to serve God, and if I
am to possess anything of " true religion," I must begin with the Substitute.   For religion begins with pardon; and without pardon religion is a

poor and irksome profession. " There
is forgiveness with Thee that Thou
mayest be feared." This is the Divine watchword. Not first the fear
of God, and then forgiveness ; but
first forgiveness, and then the fear
of God.

# THE "LONG TIME"

—*o*—

It is the Lord Jesus Himself who
has given us these words in one of
His parables. He says: "After a long
time the Lord of those servants cometh, and reckoneth with them" (Matt.
xxv. 19). Thus, while in one place
He speaks of "the little while," in
another He speaks of "the long time."
Little, yet great; short, yet long; both
are true; and it is this double expression that makes up the full character
of man's condition here, as preparing
for the great day of the Lord. From
the day when the Master left the
earth and went up to the Father, to

the day when He shall come again in
His glory to sit on the awful throne
before which all nations shall be gathered, is, in one sense, a long time, as
men reckon years and ages. But in
another sense, it is but a little while,
if we reckon time as God reckons it,
and compare it with the vast eternity
in which it is to be swallowed up.

Life is a vapor, and that is little; life
is a journey, and that is long. Life
is a hand-breadth, and that is little;
life is a period made of many days,
and weeks, and months, and years,
and that is long. Life is a post, and
that is swift; life is a pilgrimage, and
that is slow. Life is like the eagle
hastening to his prey; life is a time
of sojourning. Life is a weaver's shut-
tle; life is fourscore years, and once
it was well nigh a thousand.

For some purposes a day is a short

time, while for others it is a long time.
In some circumstances a year is a
short time, while in others it is a very
long time. Much depends upon what
is to be done in that period, and our
ideas of long and short, in such cases,
are influenced by the amount of work
to be done. "It seemed an age," said
a traveller among the Alps, who lay
bruised by a fall into a deep cleft of
ice, "ere my guides returned from the
village, bringing the ropes to pull me
up." Yet it was only two hours. But
he had measured the time, not by moments or minutes, but by his sufferings
and his danger.

Of an old German peasant the fol-
lowing story is told by a lady who
visited him. He had a little garden
in which were a few apple trees which
were covered with fruit. He amused
himself daily with walking through his

garden and picking up the apples which dropped. The lady met him one day when he was thus engaged.

"Don't you weary, my friend," said she, "stooping so often?"

"No, no," said he, smiling, and offering a handful of ripe fruit.

"I don't weary," he added: "I'm just waiting, waiting. I think I'm getting ripe now, and I must soon be dropping; and then the Lord will pick me up. Oh," said he, speaking earnestly to the lady, "you are young yet—just in blossom; turn well round to the Sun of Righteousness, that you may ripen well."

Here was the "long time" of growing and of ripening; not long in one sense, but long in another; long enough to grow and grow; long enough to ripen and ripen. It is of a "long time" like this that the Lord speaks to us in this parable of the servants.

The Italian poet, imprisoned cruelly in a dark cell, is represented as uttering these mournful words: "Long years, long years." For so they seemed to him in his sad solitude. And in a like sense we often use the words, "all day long," and "all night long," and also "the whole long year;" and thus the word "long" has acquired a peculiar meaning, expressing not only the real amount of time, but the number of events that have been crowded into the space: as if the trials passed had lengthened out the time.

It is to this solemn sense of the expression, "After a long time," that we now turn the reader's thoughts. We wish to make him feel the responsibility which is laid upon every man by the "long time" given to us by God to prepare for the coming eternity.

God will take no one by surprise. He is too just and too pitiful to do so. He warns before He strikes; nay, He gives a thousand warnings, even during the shortest life. Each day is made up of warnings, too plain to be mistaken, too loud to be unheard. No one, in the great day of reckoning, shall be able to say, "I was not told of what was coming; I was hurried off to the judgment-seat, without notice given, or time allowed to make ready." A pilot that runs his vessel upon the rocks at noonday, with his eyes open to see the cliffs, and his ears open to hear the breakers, is without excuse. At St. Abb's Head, on the east coast of Scotland, many a vessel in former years was shipwrecked when the strong east wind of the German Ocean drove it upon the treacherous lee shore. Some years

ago a lighthouse was built and a curi-
ous "fog-horn" set up, which in mist,
whether by day or night, makes its
warning voice to be heard for miles
around.  No pilot now, who wrecks
his vessel on these terrible rocks, can
say, " I got no warning that they were
so near;" for in the clear night the
beacon-light shines out to tell him
of danger, and in the thick gray mist
the " fog-horn " sounds out its hoarse
note to say, " Beware!"  Thus the
light and the voice from heaven are
perpetually warning the sons of men,
and saying, " Prepare to meet thy
God."  The warnings of one day or
one week, how many! the warnings
of a year, how many more! the warnings of a lifetime, how innumerable!
No man shall be able to say that he
perished unwarned, or that God took
him by surprise.  The " fog-horn "

pealing through the haze sounds dismally, and seems like the voice of one crying in the wilderness, "Flee from the wrath to come;" "Repent, repent;" "Turn ye, turn ye; for why will ye die?" And thus it is that God is each day calling aloud to us, and pointing us from the rocks to the haven of safety in Jesus Christ our Lord,—the one haven which no storm can reach.

God gives us time enough to turn and live. When a teacher sets a task of a few pages to his scholar, and says, "I give you a week to do it in," he allows him a "long time," for the task is one which might be done in an hour. So, when God says, "Seek ye Me, and ye shall live," or "Acquaint thyself now with God, and be at peace," and gives us a lifetime for this, He is giving us "a long time." We delay,

and linger, and loiter: so that year
after year passes by, and we are no
nearer God than at first. But our de-
lays do not change the long time.
We make it a short one by our folly;
but it was really long for the thing
that was to be done—the single step
that was to bring us to Christ and
place us beneath the shadow of His
cross. For that there was time enough,
even in the shortest life; so that no one
can say at last, "I had no time given
me to prepare for eternity, and I was
hurried to the grave without time to
seek the Lord." "I gave her space
to repent" (Rev. ii. 21), are the warning words addressed to the sinners
of Thyatira; and He speaks the same
words to us. Space to repent is the
message still! Repent is the burden
of exhortation, and this He follows up
with, "I give you space to repent!"

This long time is a time of long-suffering. "The Lord is very pitiful, and of tender mercy" (Jas. v. 11). He spares to the uttermost; He yearns over the sinner; He beseeches him, with all the earnestness and sincerity of God, to be reconciled to Himself. He bears refusals, insults, and provocation, hatred, and scorn, and cold-ness,—not smiting the rejector of His love, nor taking vengeance on His enemies. He is "not easily provoked," but "beareth all things, endureth all things:" "not willing that any should perish, but that all should come to repentance" (2 Pet. iii. 9). He renews each day His offer of pardon, with a long-suffering that seems to know no limit, and with a profound sincerity that is fitted to win the most obdurate and suspicious of the sons of men. "Account that the long-suf-

fering of the Lord is salvation;" for
to nothing less than salvation does
this long-suffering point! "Why will
ye die?" is the urgent question of
God to the heedless sinner. Have
I not given you time enough to seek
and find eternal life? Am I not in
earnest in beseeching you to be reconciled to Myself?

This long time is man's opportunity. Is pardon to be found? Now is
the time! Is eternal life to be obtained? Now is the time! Is heaven
to be won? Now is the time! Is the
strait gate to be entered and the nar-
row way to be pursued? Now is the
time! Is the immortal soul to be
saved, a crown to be received, and a
kingdom to be possessed? Now is
the time! Is the chain to be broken,
the prison to be fled from, the darkness to be exchanged for light, and the

everlasting woe to be shunned? Now is the time! This is thy opportunity, O man! Seize it, and use it, ere it pass away for ever! There is danger all around; hell is laying its snares; the storm is gathering; but still there is time. All heaven is shining yonder, full in view; the door is as wide open as the love of God can throw it; the Son of God entreats you; angels beckon you in; the earthly ambassadors beseech you; now is your opportunity;—will you let it slip? Is it such a trifle to lose heaven, to lose your soul, to lose eternal gladness? O man, delay not!

This long time will end at last. The Master will return, and call His servants to account for the way in which they have spent the time, and used the gifts. The acceptable year of the Lord will end in the day of vengeance: and that vengeance will be real, for it is the vengeance of God. The "long time" allowed us here, to prepare for the great reckoning, will be nothing to the far longer time of the unending eternity,—an eternity of ever deepening darkness, or ever brightening glory.

All this makes us speak more earnestly, knowing how quickly the "long time" is passing away. Time is closing, life is ending, the Judge is coming; the long time will melt into the "little while"; the "little while" will vanish away, and the everlasting ages will begin. Prepare to meet thy God. Lately, when making alterations in an English church, an old pulpit was found, that had been hidden for long years. It was beautifully carved, and round its upper part these words were cut in the wood, still distinctly legible,—

" Lift up thy voice like a trumpet, cry aloud." It is this that we are now doing, that every one to whom this may come may know the danger which lies in front of him, if he be still un-reconciled to God.

There is reconciliation! This is our message, as we stand beneath the cross, and speak to a dying world. There is reconciliation through the blood of the sacrifice! there is peace at the altar where God is standing to receive the sinner. The Son of God has done the mighty work on which reconcilia-tion rests, and by means of which the eternal friendship of God is offered to the oldest and most stubborn of earth's rebels. That word supersedes all others. It is enough! Do not at-tempt to add to it, or to take from it. Take it for what it is; take it for what God declares it to be, and enter into the purchased peace. It is a righteous peace, built upon the finished work of the Substitute. It tells of that God who "justifies the ungodly," and it tells of that peace-offering by means of which it has become a righteous thing that the ungodly should be justified. It says to each rebel,—All this peace, this friendship, this pardon becomes the certain and present property of every one who relinquishes his own standing by nature before God in himself, and consents to stand before Him on the footing of another's work, another's sufferings,—the work and the sufferings of the Word made flesh; of Him who, though He was rich, yet for our sakes became poor, that we through His poverty might be rich (2 Cor. viii. 9).

# I CAN'T LET GO

—o—

THE vessel was pretty high out of the water, and there was no ladder, either of rope or iron, at his side for the poor lad to descend by, so as to reach the boat which lay below.

The lad looked over and saw his position. There was the boat, and here was the slowly sinking vessel. He heard shouts to him from below; he saw some five or six stout men waiting to catch him; but he could not make up his mind to quit his hold.

He saw the swell of the sea, as it heaved the boat up and down; he observed, too, the distance between himself and his deliverers below; and his heart failed him. What if he should miss the boat, and drop into the sea, instead of the stretched-out arms underneath? He clung to the rope with all his might, and made as though he would go back into the vessel. But the shouts came up again, "Let go the rope!" He dared not go back, and he was afraid to let himself drop. So he clung to the rope as if it were his only safety. Again the shouts were heard, "Let go!" His answer was, "I can't let go."

At last, as the danger increased, the loud but kindly voices from below overcame his fear and distrust. He did "let go"; and without an effort dropped into the strong arms which were waiting to receive him. He was safe; and as he realized his safety, he could not help smiling at his own folly in refusing to let go, and in saying, as his resaon for not letting go, that he could not.

"I can't believe in Christ," is the complaint we often hear from the inquiring. What does it mean? Are those who make it in earnest? Have they considered what they say? Are they not exactly like the poor lad hanging over the steamer's side and crying "I can't let go?" If he had had confidence in the boat below and in the men below, would he have remained in this strange position and uttering this strange cry? Had he not more confidence in the rope to which he clung than in the boat which lay ready to receive him? He saw there was danger, or he would not have grasped the rope; but he had the feeling that there was less danger in

clinging to the rope than in dropping
into the boat. So he continued, to
cling with all his might to that which
could not save. If his safety had depended upon his grasping it, the cry,
" I can't hold any longer, my strength
is gone," would have been most nat-
ural and intelligible; but, when his
safety depended upon his ceasing to
cling to that which could not save,
and simply drop into that which could
save, the cry was foolish and untrue.

So is it with the complaint of the
anxious to which we have referred.
They do not see the open door of the
ark, the stretched-out arms of the Deliverer. It is that Deliverer who cries
to them, " Let go; I am waiting with
open arms to receive you." But they
seem to think that He is commanding
them to do some great thing, to put
forth some prodigious exertion of their

own strength; and so they reply to all
His messages of grace, "I can't, I
can't!" He sees them clinging to
self with all their might; and He says,
"Let go, let go;" but they reply, "We
can't!" Is not this folly? Is it not
a rejection of His finished work?

Suppose, when Jesus called to Zac-
cheus to come down from his syca-
more, the publican had replied, "I
can't!" what would he have meant?
Had the Lord bidden him climb the
tree, he might have said, perhaps, "I
can't!" but when Christ says "Come
down!" the excuse would have been
absurd.

Suppose when the father, in receiving back the prodigal, had said,
"Go into the house, and get the best
robe and put it on and come to me,"
there might have been some meaning in the son's saying, "I can't!"

But when the father says to the servants, "Bring forth the best robe and *put it on* him," such an excuse would have been absurd, and would only have betrayed the son's unwillingness to receive the robe at all. For the father leaves nothing for the son to *do;* all he desires is that he should *receive:* and it is as if he had said, "Allow me to clothe you; allow me to put the best robe upon you." He undertakes for everything; for the *putting on* the robe as well as for the robe itself.

That which many call the difficulty of believing is the essence of self-righteousness. Yes; it is this that lies at the root of, or rather *is* the root of, this difficulty. Men cling to *self* as the lad clung to the rope; they will not let it go; and they cry all the while that they can't.

I admit the difficulty. It is a root
of bitterness. But it is far deeper
than many think. It is far worse and
more serious than those who speak of
it will admit. It is man's determined
*self-righteousness* that really constitutes
the difficulty. He is unwilling to let
this go; and he says "I can't!" to
cover over the guilt of the "I won't!"

Deep down in man's depraved being lies this awful evil, which only
God can remove, this determination
not to give up self. He deceives himself sadly in this matter, in order to
cover his guilt and to pass the blame
of his unbelief on God. He holds
that he has some great thing to *do:*
though God has declared a hundred
times over that *the great thing* is done!
He wants to do the great thing, and
to get the credit of doing it; and because God has declared that the great

thing is done, "once for all," never
to be done again, he retires into himself, and tries to get up another great
thing within himself, by the right doing of which he will please God and
satisfy his own conscience. *Acceptance
of the great thing done* is what God
presses on him as altogether and absolutely sufficient for his salvation and
his peace. But this he shrinks from.
He thinks he must wait, and work,
and struggle, and weep before he is
in a fit state for accepting; and therefore it is that he replies to all the
messages from the "ambassadors of
peace," "I can't." He won't do that
which God wishes him to do; he sub-
stitutes something else of his own,
some process of preparation for acceptance : and because he finds he makes
no progress in this work of "voluntary
humility," he says, "I can't!"

God brings him face to face with
the cross, saying, "Look and live!"
But he thinks this too simple, and he
turns away seeking for something to
*do!* God sets the fountain before
him, and says, "Wash." He says, "I
cannot," and turns away to something
else. God brings him the best robe,
the righteousness of the Righteous
One, and offers to put it on. But this
is too simple. It leaves nothing for
him to *do*—nothing but to be clothed
by another's hand in another's rai-
ment. And so, in pretended humility, he postpones the acceptance of
the robe, under the plea that he cannot put it on! God brings him face
to face with His free love, and says,
"Take this and be at rest." But as
this still takes for granted that *the great
thing is done*, in virtue of which this
free love is to flow into the sinner,

and that God now wants him simply to recognize this great work and its completeness, in order to his acceptance, he hesitates or turns wholly from the Divine proposal, refusing to let the love flow in, just because it is so absolutely free! He resembles the Syrian general whom Elisha told to wash in Jordan that his leprosy might be healed. "Naaman was wroth, and went away, and said, Behold, I thought he will surely come out to me, and stand, and call on the name of the Lord his God, and strike his hand over the place, and recover the leper. Are not Abana and Pharpar, rivers of Damascus, better than all the waters of Israel? may I not wash in them, and be clean? So he turned and went away in a rage."* And may we not address him in the words

* 2 Kings v. 11, 12.

of the servants on that occasion: " If
the prophet had bid thee do some
great thing, wouldest thou not have
done it? how much rather then, when
he saith to thee, Wash, and be clean?"

The simplicity of the gospel, however, does not lessen man's depravity,
nor supersede the necessity for the
power of the Holy Ghost.  It is in
reference to this free gospel that man's
" evil heart of unbelief " has always ex-
hibited itself most strongly.   The gospel is simple, faith is simple, the Word
is simple, the way is simple, the cross
is simple; but man's heart is wholly
set against these.   He resists and re-
fuses.   He prefers some way of his
own, and he casts the blame of his
own evil upon God.

Hence the need for the Holy Spirit,
by whose hand the Almighty works
upon the human soul in ways so unseen

and simple that, when the man has at
length believed, he wonders how he
could so long have stood aloof and
resisted such a gospel. To disarm the
enmity, to remove the hardness, to
open the eye, and to renew the will,
the Spirit operates. " The wind blow-
eth where it listeth, and " we cannot
" tell whence it cometh, and whither
it goeth: so is every one that is born
of the Spirit."

It is man's deep depravity and total
alienation from God that makes the
power of the Almighty Spirit indis-
pensable for his renewal. But it is
of great importance that he should
not be allowed to make use of that
depravity as an excuse for not returning to God, or to abuse the doc-
trine of the Spirit's work by making it a reason for cleaving to self,
and refusing to believe the gospel;

as if he were more willing to be
wrought upon than the Spirit is to
work, or as if he wanted to believe,
but the Spirit would not help him.

It was man's *guilt* that rendered
the cross necessary; for if that guilt
remained unremoved, all else would
be vain. To be *under condemnation*
would be to be shut out of the kingdom for ever. To have the Judge
of all against him in the great day
would be certain doom. The cross
has come to lift off that guilt from
us, and to lay it upon another; upon
Him who is able to bear it all; upon
Him who is mighty to save. That
which should have come upon the
sinner has come upon Him, that the
sinner might go free. The Judge is
satisfied with the work done on Cal-
vary, and asks no more: and when
the sinner is brought by the Holy

Spirit to be satisfied with that which
has satisfied the Judge, the chains that
bound the burden to his shoulders
snap, and the burden falls, to disappear
for ever—buried in the grave of the
Substitute, from which it cannot rise.

# WHITHER? WHITHER?

—o—

In the beginning of last century, an old American Christian died, leaving on his death-bed this message to his son,—" Remember that there is A LONG ETERNITY."

But this was not all. He laid upon his family the dying command, that the same message should be handed down to the next generation, and from that to the next again, as long as any of his posterity remained. The command was obeyed. One generation after another received the solemn message, " Remember there is *a long eter-*

*nity.*" And the words, we are told, bore fruit in the conversion of children, and grandchildren, and great-grandchildren.

It is of this *long eternity* that God so often speaks to us in His book, with the words "everlasting," "without end," "for ever and for ever." It is of this *long eternity* that each death-bed speaks to us,—each shroud, each coffin, each grave. It is of this *long eternity* that each closing and opening year speaks to us, pointing forward to the endless years which lie beyond the brief days of time,—brief days which are hurrying us without slackening to the life or to the death which must be the issue of all things on earth. Of that eternity we may say that its years shall be as many as the leaves of the forest, or as the sands of the sea-shore, or as the drops of the ocean,

or as the stars of heaven, or as the
blades of grass, or as the sparkles of
dew, all multiplied together.   And who
can reckon up these numbers, or con-
ceive the prodigious sum,—millions
upon millions of ages.

A traveller, some years ago, tells
that in the room of a hotel where he
lodged there was hung a large printed
sheet, with these solemn words:—

> "Know these things, O Man,—
> A GOD, a Moment, an Eternity."

Surely it would be our wisdom to
think on words like these,—so brief,
yet so full of meaning.

Richard Baxter mentions the case
of a minister of his day, the whole
tone of whose life-preaching was affected by the words which he heard
when visiting a dying woman, who
"often and vehemently" (he says)

"did cry out" on her death-bed, "Oh,
call time back again, call time back
again!" But the calling of time back
again is as hopeless as the shortening
of eternity. "This inch of hasty time,"
as that noble preacher calls it, cannot
be lengthened out; and if not improved
or redeemed, is lost for ever. While
God lives, the soul must live; for "in
Him we live, and move, and have our
being."

Our internal future is no dream nor
fable. It will be as real as our past
has been,—nay, more so. Unbelief
may try to persuade us that it is a
shadow or a fancy. But it is not. It
is infinitely and unutterably real; and
the ages before us, as they come and
go, will bring with them realities in
comparison with which all past realities will be as nothing. All things
pertaining to us are becoming every

day more real; and this increase of reality shall go on through the ages to come.

*Whither? whither?* This is no idle question; and it is one to which every son of man ought to seek an immediate answer. Man was made that he might look into the long future; and this question is one which he ought to know how to put, and how to answer. If he does not there must be something sadly wrong about him. For God has not denied him the means of replying to it aright.

*Whither? whither?* Child of mortality, dost thou not know? dost thou not care to know? Is it no concern of thine to discover what thy existence is to be, and where thou art to spend eternity? Thy all is wrapped up in it; and dost thou not care?

*Whither? whither?* Dost thou hate

the question? Does it disturb thy re-
pose, and mar thy pleasures? Does
it fret thy conscience, and cast a
shadow over life? Yet, whether thou
hatest or lovest it, thou must one day
be brought face to face with it. Thou
shall one day put it, and answer it.
Perhaps, when thou art putting it and
trying to answer it, the Judge may
come, and the last trumpet sound.
" While they went to buy, the Bride-
groom came."

*Whither? whither?* Ask the falling leaf. It says, "I know not." Ask
the restless wind. It says, "I know
not." Ask the foam upon the wave.
It says, "I know not." But man is
none of these. He is bound to look
into his prospects, and to ascertain
*whither he is going*. He is not a
leaf, or a cloud, or a breeze, not knowing whence they come and whither

they go.  He *knows* that there is a
future of some kind before him, and
that into that future he must ere long
enter.   What is it to be to him?
That is the question!

*Whither? whither?*   Go to yon
harbor, where some score of vessels
are lying, just preparing to start.  Go
up to the captain and ask, Whither
bound?  Will he answer, "I know
not"?  Go to yon railway station and
ask the guard of the train just moving
off, Whither bound?   Will he say, "I
know not"?  No; these men have
more wisdom than to go whither they
know not, or to set out on a journey
without concerning themselves about
its end.  Shall the children of time
be able to answer such questions as
to their route and destination, and
shall a child of eternity go on in
the dark, heedless of the shadows

into which he is passing, and resting his immortality upon a mere perchance?

But can I get an answer to this question here? Can I secure my eternity while here on earth? and can I so know that I have secured it that I shall be able to say, "I am on my way to the kingdom: let this present life be long or short, the eternal life is mine?"

The gospel which God has given us is that by which we are enabled to answer the question, "*Whither? whither?*" for it shows us the way to the kingdom,—a way not far off, but near; a way not inaccessible, but most accessible; a way not costly, but free; a way not for the good, but for the evil; a way not hidden, but plain and clear. "The wayfaring man, though a fool, shall not err therein." He whom the Father has sent to be "the Saviour of the world" says, "I am the way."

The knowledge of that way is everything to us: for he who knows it, knows whither he is going; and he who knows it not, knows not whither he is going. The right and sure answer to the question, "Whither?" depends entirely on our true knowledge of the way. For the world is dark, and can tell us nothing of the way; nor can it in the least enable us to answer the awful question, "Whither am I going, with all these sins of mine, and with a judgment day in prospect, and with the certainty that I must give an account of the deeds done in the body?"

In order, then, to get the answer to the question we must come at once to the "good news,"—the glad tid-

ings which God has sent to us concerning Him who "died for our sins,
according to the Scriptures;" "who
was buried and rose again." It is the
belief of this good news that *connects
us with Him;* and in so doing, enables
us to answer the question, "Whither
am I going?" For if we are *connected with Him*, then assuredly we
are going where He has gone before
us. By the belief of the gospel we
are brought into possession of that
everlasting life which He has secured
for sinners by His death upon the
cross, as the propitiation for sin.

We knew one who, filled with dread
of the unknown future, sought for years
to get an answer to the question as
to his own eternal prospects. He labored, and prayed, and strove, expecting that God would have pity upon
his earnest efforts, and give him what

he sought. At the end of many long, weary years, he came to see, that what he had been thus laboring to do, in order to win God's favor, another had already done, and done far better than he could ever do. He saw that what he had been laboring for years to persuade God to give him, might have been had, at the very outset, simply by believing the good news that there was no need for all this long waiting, and working, and praying; and that now, at last, by receiving the Divine testimony to the person and work of the Only-begotten of the Father, he could count with certainty upon the favor of God to himself, as one who had believed the record which God had given of His Son (1 John v. 10–12). Thus believing "he entered into rest,"—the present rest of soul which is the result of a believed gos-

pel, and the earnest of the future
rest which remaineth for the people
of God.

To say to any sinner that he
must answer that momentous question, " Whither? " and yet not to tell
him the Divine provision made for his
answering it, would be only to mock
him. But to call on him for an answer, while making known to him the
grace of Christ and the open way to
God, is to gladden his soul, by showing how he may at once find the
means of answering it, without working, or waiting, or qualifying himself
for securing the favor of God.

To the troubled spirit, we hold forth
the free and immediate pardon which
the gospel places in our hands,—*a
pardon which no prayers or exertions
of ours can make more free*, or more
near; a pardon flowing directly from

the finished propitiation of the cross; a pardon for the ungodly and the unworthy; a pardon which, while it glorifies Him who pardons, brings immediate liberty and deliverance to the pardoned one. "Through this Man is preached unto you the forgiveness of sins; and by Him ALL THAT BELIEVE ARE JUSTIFIED" (Acts xiii. 38, 39). If justified, then we know our *future* as well as our *present;* for "whom He justifies, them He also glorifies" (Rom. viii. 30).

"It is all dark," said a dying young man who had trifled with the great question throughout life. "I'm awfully afraid," was the language of another in similar circumstances. "I have provided for everything but death," said an old general, as he was passing away. "No mercy for me," was the death-bed cry of one who in early life had promised well, but had gone utterly back. "I'm dying," said another, "and I don't know where I'm going." Such death-beds are sorrowful indeed. Darkness overshadows them. No ray of hope brightens the gloom.

But he who has accepted the great salvation is lifted above these fears and uncertainties. The light of the cross shines down upon him, and he looks into the vast future without alarm. "I know whom I have believed," he says; "and knowing Him, I know where I am going. I am going to spend an eternity with Him whom, not having seen, I love. I am going to the city which hath foundations; and though worms may destroy this body, yet in my flesh shall I see God." The question "Whither?" has no terrors to him. He knows that all is well. Eternity is to him a word

of joy.   He has believed; and he is
sure that his faith will not be put
to shame.   The simple word of the
Son of God, "He that believeth is
not condemned," suffices for him to
rest upon, in life and in death.

## "THE WORLD PASSETH AWAY"

—o—

THE things that are seen are temporal. Ours is a dying world, and here we have no continuing city. But a few years,—it may be less,—and all things here are changed. But a few years,—it may be less,—and the Lord shall have come, and the last trumpet shall have sounded, and the great sentence shall have been pronounced upon each of the sons of men.

There is a world that passeth not away. It is fair and glorious. It is called "the inheritance in light." It is bright with the love of God, and with the joy of heaven. "The Lamb is

the light thereof." Its gates are of
pearl; they are always open. And as
we tell men of this wondrous city, we
tell them to enter in.

The Book of Revelation (chap. xviii.
21, 22) tells us the story of earth's
vanity: "A mighty angel took up a
stone like a great millstone, and cast
it into the sea, saying, Thus with vi-
olence shall that great city Babylon
be thrown down, and shall be found
no more at all. And the voice of
harpers and musicians, and of pipers
and trumpeters, shall be heard no more
at all in thee. And no craftsman, of
whatsoever craft he be, shall be found
any more in thee."

Such is the day that is coming on
the world, and such is the doom over-
hanging earth,—a doom dimly fore-
shadowed by the sad commercial dis-
asters that have often sent sorrow into

so many hearts, and desolation into so many homes.

An old minister—now two hundred years since—lay dying. His fourscore years were well-nigh completed. He had been tossed on many a wave, from England to America, from America to England, again from England to America. At Boston he lay dying, full of faith and love. The evening before his death, as he lay all but speechless, his daughter asked him how it was with him. He lifted up his dying hands, and with his dying lips simply said, " Vanishing things, vanishing things!" We repeat his solemn words, and, pointing to the world, with all the vanities on which vain man sets his heart, say, " Vanishing things!"

" The world passeth away." This is our message.

Like a dream of the night. We lie

down to rest; we fall asleep; we dream; we awake at morn; and lo, all is fled that in our dream seemed so stable and so pleasant! So hastes the world away. O child of mortality, have you no brighter world beyond?

Like the mist of the morning. The night brings down the mists upon the hills,—the vapor covers the valleys; the sun rises, all has passed off,—hill and vale are clear. So the world passeth off, and is seen no more. O man, will you embrace a world like this? Will you lie down upon a mist, and say, This is my home?

Like a shadow. There is nothing more unreal than a shadow. It has no substance, no being. It is dark, it is a figure, it has motion, that is all! Such is the world. O man will you chase a shadow? What will a shadow do for you?

Like a wave of the sea. It rises,
falls, and is seen no more. Such is
the history of a wave. Such is the
story of the world. O man will you
make a wave your portion? Have
you no better pillow on which to
lay your wearied head than this? A
poor world this for human heart to
love, for an immortal soul to be filled
with!

Like a rainbow. The sun throws
its colors on a cloud, and for a few
minutes all is brilliant. But the cloud
shifts, and the brilliance is all gone.
Such is the world. With all its beauty
and brightness; with all its honors
and pleasures; with all its wealth and
greatness; with all its mirth and mad-
ness; with all its pomp and luxury;
with all its revelry and riot; with all
its hopes and flatteries; with all its
love and laughter; with all its songs

and splendor; with all its gems and gold,—it vanishes. And the cloud that knew the rainbow knows it no more. O man, is a passing world like this all that you have for an inheritance?

Like a flower. Beautiful, very beautiful; fragrant, very fragrant, are the summer flowers. But they wither away. So fades the world from before our eyes. While we are looking at it, and admiring it, behold, it is gone! No trace is left of all its loveliness but a little dust! O man, can you feed on flowers? Can you dote on that which is but for an hour? You were made for eternity; and only that which is eternal can be your portion or your resting-place. The things that perish with the using only mock your longings. They cannot fill you; and even if they filled, they cannot abide. Mortality is written on all things here; immor-

tality belongs only to the world to
come,—to that new heavens and new
earth wherein dwelleth righteousness.

Like a ship at sea. With all ·its
sails set, and a fresh breeze blowing,
the vessel comes into sight, passes
before our eye in the distance, and
then disappears. So comes, so goes,
so vanishes away this present world,
with all that it contains. A few hours
within sight, then gone! The wide
sea o'er which it sailed as calm or as
stormy as before; no trace anywhere of
all the life or motion or beauty which
was passing over it! O man, is that
vanishing world thy only dwelling-
place? Are all thy treasures, thy
hopes, thy joys laid up there? Where
will all these be when thou goest down
to the tomb? Or where wilt thou be,
when these things leave thee, and thou
art stripped of all the inheritance which

thou art ever to have for eternity? It is a poor heritage at the best, and its short duration makes it poorer still. Oh, choose the better part, which shall not be taken from thee!

Like a tent in the desert. They who have travelled over the Arabian sands know what this means. At sunset a little speck of white seems to rise out of the barren waste. It is a traveller's tent. At sunrise it disappears. Both it and its inhabitant are gone. The wilderness is as lonely as before. Such is the world. To-day it shows itself; to-morrow it disappears. O man, born of a woman, is that thy stay and thy home? Wilt thou say of it, "This is my rest," when we tell you that there is a rest, an everlasting rest, remaining for the people of God?

THE WORLD PASSETH AWAY. This is

the message from heaven. All flesh is grass, and all the goodliness thereof as the flower of the field.

THE WORLD PASSETH AWAY. But God ever liveth. He is from everlasting to everlasting; the King eternal and immortal.

THE WORLD PASSETH AWAY. But man is immortal. Eternity lies before each son of Adam as the duration of his lifetime. In light or in darkness for ever! In joy or in sorrow for ever!

THE WORLD PASSETH AWAY. What then? This is the question that so deeply concerns man. If the world is to vanish away, and man is to live for ever, of what importane is it to know where and what we are to be for ever! A celebrated physician, trying to cheer a desponding patient, said to him, "Treat life as a plaything." It was wretched counsel. For life is no plaything, and time is no child's toy, to be flung away. Life here is the beginning of the life which has no end; and time is but the gateway of eternity.

What then? Thou must, O man, make sure of a home in that world into which thou art so soon to pass. Thou must not pass out of this tent without making sure of the city which hath foundations, whose builder and maker is God. When thou hast done this thou canst lie down upon thy death-bed in peace. Till thou hast done this, thou canst neither live nor die in peace. One who had lived a worldly life at last lay down to die; and when about to pass away he uttered these terrible words, "I am dying, and I don't know where I am going." Another in similar circumstances cried out, "I am within an hour of eternity, and all is dark." O man of earth, it is time to awake!

"How can I make sure?" you ask. God has long since answered that question, and His answer is recorded for all ages: "Believe on the Lord Jesus Christ, and thou shalt be saved."

"Believe on the Lord Jesus Christ! I have never done anything else," you say. If that be really true, then, as the Lord liveth, thou art a saved man. But is it really so? Has thy life been the life of a saved man? No, verily. It has been a life wholly given to vanity. Then as the Lord God of Israel liveth, and as thy soul liveth, thou hast not believed, and thou art not yet saved.

"Have I then no work to work in this great matter of my pardon?" None. What work canst thou work? What work of thine can buy forgiveness, or make thee fit for the Divine favor? What work has God bidden thee work in order to obtain salvation? None. His Word is very plain, and easy to be understood: "To him that worketh not, but believeth in Him that justifieth the ungodly, his faith is counted for righteousness" (Rom. iv. 5).

There is but one work by which a man can be saved. That work is not thine, but the work of the Son of God. That work is finished,—neither to be taken from nor added to,—perfect through all ages,—and presented by Himself to you, that you may avail yourself of it and be saved.

"And is that work available for me just as I am?" It is. God has brought it to your door; and your only way of honoring it is by accepting it for yourself, and taking it as

the one basis of your eternal hope.
We honor the Father when we consent to be saved entirely by the finished work of His Son; and we honor
the Son when we consent to take His
one finished work in room of all our
works; and we honor the Holy Spirit,
whose office is to glorify Christ, when
we hear what He saith to us concerning that work finished "once for all"
upon the cross.

Forgiveness through the man Christ
Jesus, who is Son of God as well as
Son of man! This is our message.
Forgiveness through the one work of
sin-bearing which He accomplished for
sinners upon earth. Forgiveness to
the worst and wickedest, to the far-
thest off from God whom this earth
contains. Forgiveness of the largest,
fullest, completest kind; without stint,
or exception, or condition, or the pos-

sibility of revocation! Forgiveness
free and undeserved,—free as the love
of God, free as the gift of His beloved
Son. Forgiveness ungrudged and un-
restrained,—whole-hearted and joyful,
as the forgiveness of the father falling
on the neck of the prodigal! Forgiveness simply in believing; for, " by
Him all that believe are justified from
all things."

Could salvation be made more free?
Could forgiveness be brought nearer?
Could God in any way more fully show
His earnest desire that you should not
be lost, but saved,—that you should
not die, but live?

In the cross there is salvation—no-
where else. No failure of this world's
hopes can quench the hope which it
reveals. It shines brightest in the
evil day. In the day of darkening
prospects, of thickening sorrows, of

heavy burdens, of pressing cares,—
when friends depart, when riches fly
away, when disease oppresses us, when
poverty knocks at our door,—then the
cross shines out, and tells us of a light
beyond this world's darkness, the Light
of Him who is the light of the world.

# WHAT IF IT BE ALL TRUE?

—o—

John Newton had a pious mother, who was taken from him when he was only seven years old. She taught him, when but an infant, to pray, and sowed in his young heart the seeds of his future spiritual life.

When a boy he was led to think much of God and of eternal things; but his impressions wore off, and he entered on a course of sin. It seemed as if he had broken loose from all bonds, and delighted only in what was evil.

While in this impenitent state he

was thrown from a horse, and was in great danger, but his life was preserved. Then his conscience awoke once more, and he trembled at the thought of appearing before God, sinful and unready. Under this dread he forsook his sins for a while, and gave up his profane living and speaking; but the reformation was only outward, and did not last long.

At another time, dread of God's wrath overtook him, and he began to live, as he thought, a very religious life. He thought to make himself righteous, and so to win God's favor. He spent much time in reading the Scriptures; he prayed; he fasted; he would hardly trust himself to speak, lest he should utter a vain or sinful word. Ignorant of God's righteousness, he was bent on having one of his own, by which he hoped to pacify

his conscience, and get quit of his
fear of coming wrath.

This state of mind lasted a year or
two, and then he gave up religion altogether, and became an infidel. He
now rushed into wickedness of every
kind; and yet he only became more
wretched. He went to sea on board
a slave ship, and took part in that
horrid trade. He was reduced to utter
poverty—starving, and sinning, and
blaspheming—his heart hard and his
conscience seared. He was in very
deed the prodigal son, wasting his
substance with riotous living, but not
yet "coming to himself," and saying,
"I will arise, and go to my father."
Once and again he was in peril of
his life by sea and land. Half-intoxi-
cated, and dancing on deck one mid-
night, his hat went overboard, and he
was throwing himself after it when laid

hold of and dragged back by his comrades. Thus he hurried on in sin, as he himself in one of his hymns describes it:

> "In evil long I took delight,
> Unawed by shame or fear."

Finding one day a religious book on board the vessel, he took it up, and looking into it, was led to ask the question, "WHAT IF THESE THINGS SHOULD BE TRUE?" The thought terrified him, and he closed the book. He went to his hammock that night as usual, having contrived to put this solemn question out of his mind. In the dark night he was awakened by the dash of waves. A storm had risen, a terrible sea had swept over the vessel, and the cabin where he lay was fast filling. The cry rose, "The ship is sinking!" All was confusion and terror. He twice made for the deck, but was met upon the ladder by the captain, who bade him bring a knife. As he was returning for the knife, a man went up in his place, and was washed away.

Thoughts of other days began to come back upon him; the remembrance of those whom he had loved affected him, and his heart seemed softening. For four weeks the vessel was tossed to and fro, he being sometimes at the helm and sometimes at the pumps, wave upon wave breaking over him. Then, in the midst of danger, day and night his cry went up, "O God, save me, or I perish;" and, "The God of the Bible forgive me for His Son's sake;" and, "My mother's God, the God of mercy, have mercy upon me."

That storm was to John Newton

what the earthquake was to the jailer at Philippi: it brought him to his knees. It brought his sins before him. It brought before him his eternal ruin. It brought him to the cross and blood of Christ. The hymn of which we have already quoted the first two lines goes on to tell his experience:

> " In evil long I took delight,
>     Unawed by shame or fear,
>  Till A NEW OBJECT struck my sight,
>     And stopped my wild career."

The " new object " which met his eye, as he stood at the helm or walked the deck, with the waves dashing over him, was the crucified Christ. The cross, and the Son of God there bearing our sins, stood out before him in the brightness of Divine love. For thus he sings:

> " I saw one hanging on a tree
>    In agonies and blood,
> Who fixed His languid eyes on me,
>    As near His cross I stood."

As it was with Simon Peter when the Lord turned and looked upon him, so was it with John Newton. In both cases the look of love melted the sinner down:

> " Sure never till my latest breath
>    Can I forget that look;
> It seemed to charge me with His death,
>    Though not a word He spoke."

That look of love, holy love, went through and through his conscience, making him feel his sin in all its vileness. *Sin*, which had hitherto been treated by him as a mere trifle, or been altogether overlooked, now presented itself in all its terrors. He was doomed; he was lost; what shall he do?

> "My conscience felt and owned the guilt,
>   And plunged me in despair;
> I saw my sins His blood had spilt,
>   And helped to nail Him there."

He is overwhelmed; he is in despair. That look of holy love has smitten him through and through. It says to him: "Thou art the man; thou didst it all; thou hast nailed Me to the tree; had it not been for thy sins, I had not been here." But as he looks, he sees something more in that look, and hears the voice of pardon coming from the cross:

> "A second look He gave, which said,
>   I freely all forgive:
> This blood is for thy ransom paid,
>   I die that thou may'st live."

This second look speaks of peace. He reads forgiveness in it—free for-giveness to the chief of sinners—for-giveness to "the old African blasphemer," and his troubled conscience is pacified. "I have found a ransom," is the message which removes his terror; and this ransom is by the blood and death of the Son of God. That ransom suffices. God looks at it and is satisfied; He says it is enough. The sinner looks at it and is satisfied; he says it is enough. The burden of guilt is unloosed, and falls from his shoulders. He is set free from guilt, from terror, from bondage. He knows the blessedness of the man whose transgression is forgiven and whose sin is covered. He has believed, and he is saved; nay, and he knows that he is saved, for he credits the heavenly record concerning Him to whom he is looking:

"Thus, while His death my sin displays
    In all its blackest hue,
  Such is the mystery of grace,
    It seals my pardon too."

Forgiveness through the blood of the Lamb—forgiveness through the belief of the Holy Spirit's testimony to the finished work of Immanuel—this is now his resting-place; and his whole life is changed. That holy pardon has made him a holy man.

And now let us come back to the first thought that struck him—

"WHAT IF ALL THIS BE TRUE?"

Here is a question for us, no less than for him.

If eternity be a reality, then it becomes me to prepare for it, for endless terror or endless joy can be no trifle. If I must live for ever, then I must seek so to live here as to make that everlasting living a happy one. Otherwise it had been good for me that I had never been born.

If sin be a fact, then I must not trifle with it; and if God hates it utterly, then I must hate it too, and I must get quit of it. And I must get quit of it in God's way, for no other way of deliverance will avail. That which is so awfully real and powerful as sin is, can only be taken away by something as real and as powerful as itself.

If the cross of Christ be true, then I must deal with it accordingly. It is meant to be the death of sin and the life of righteousness. It is meant to be the fountain opened for sin and for uncleanness. It is meant to be the place where all sin is borne by another for us, so that we live by the death of another, and are pardoned by the condemnation of another. My acceptance of the great work done there is my deliverance from wrath, and sin, and death. I am not bidden to *work* for pardon: I get it freely, and without desert. I am not bidden to *wait* for pardon: I get it at once as a finished and provided gift, bestowed upon every one who will go to God for it, and take it in His appointed way.

If all these things be true, then I must be *in earnest*. Everything connected with God and Christ, with sin and pardon, with life and death, with wrath and favor, with time and eternity, is so unspeakably momentous, that I must be up and minding these things without delay. If I am not in earnest, I am a fool; for what shall it profit me to gain the whole world and to lose my soul? I must seek the right thing. I must seek it at the right time. I must seek it in the right way, I must go straight to God for all I want; and I must meet Him at the cross.

I knew one who was all his life seeking, and yet he never seemed to find. He was trying to be happy, but knew not how. He was rich, and had everything that this world could give him. He went about from place to place in search of pleasure. He lived a long life, and spent it in the midst of luxury, eating and drinking and making merry. He had broad lands; he had many friends; and his house was filled with pictures, and statues, and everything that art could provide for him. Yet his weary eye told you that he was not happy. Life seemed to have no joy in it; and yet every day, from morning to night, he was going about in quest of joy. " Who will show me any good? " was his cry. But the good never came. He passed through life weary and unhappy, though apparently possessing all its pleasures.

He died about the age of fourscore, and he did not seem ever to have known a happy day. He lived in vain, both for himself and others.

My friend, would you be *happy?* You must go to God for His love and joy. This world, with riches and pleasures to the full, will do nothing for you. It cannot give you peace. But the God who made you can give you peace—His own satisfying peace. Go *immediately*, and get it from Him. He giveth to all liberally, and upbraideth not.

Would you be *safe?* You must seek your safety in the Son of God, and beneath the protection of His cross. In Him only you are safe. His cross is a shield and hiding-place for time and eternity. Time will soon pass away: the last trumpet may soon sound, and you must stand before the

judgment-seat of Christ, to give account of the deeds done in the body.
Seek *immediate safety* in Christ Jesus,
the Lamb of God, who taketh away
the sin of the world. He is able to
save to the uttermost them that come
unto God by Him. He waits to welcome the guilty. He loves to bless
the sinner. Go to Him now, and deal
with Him fully, and fervently, and hon-
estly, about that soul of yours. He
will not send you empty away.

# THE AGES TO COME

—o—

"The ages to come!" What are they to be to me? How long are they to last?

We pass into the new year asking these questions; for our days move on with speed; our life is brief; its end is getting nearer; and we seem sometimes to get a glimpse of the burying-place where we may soon be laid, and almost to read our names upon the stone, with the text beneath: "As for man, his days are as grass; as a flower of the field, so he flour-isheth: for the wind passeth over it, and it is gone; and the place thereof shall know it no more" (Psalm ciii. 15, 16).

Very near has death come to us during the past year. Loud have been his knocks at our door. His trumpet has given no uncertain sound. Six hundred sleepers in one minute sink beneath the wave, as the blast seizes one of our strongest war vessels and plunges it into the deep as if it were a child's toy. Some of these sleepers were ready. From their sinking vessel the eternal life-boat carried them at once to their desired haven, and the ship was at the land whither they went (John vi. 21); for them that sleep in Jesus will God bring with Him (1 Thess. iv. 14). Others might not be ready, and no time was left them to prepare; not even the brief time of common ship-wreck; not even the few hours given to the thief upon the cross.

Prepare then, O man, to meet thy God!

The governor of Paris lately requested the German commander to give notice of the time when the bombardment of the " joyous city" would begin. The German refused. No warning is to be given. In an unexpected moment, when Paris is perhaps least expecting it, the circle of dormant fire will blaze out, and the awful death-shower commence. So, O man, shall it be with thee. In vain thou askest for some warning, some intimation of thy coming foe. There shall no sign be given, but the signs that are common to all; and these, perhaps, thou art at this moment slighting. It is never too late, indeed, to look to the brazen serpent, so long as the living eye can, even dimly, see the glorious Healer. It

is never too late to betake thyself,
with all thy sins, to the gracious " Son
of the Highest," so long as thou art
on this side of the deep gulf.  It is
never too late, whilst thou art here,
to wash in the blood, to put on the
righteousness, to receive the pardon,
to drink of the water of life.  But
how unlikely is it, that they who have
forgotten these things in life will remember them when the darkness of
a dying hour is over them.  How difficult, even if they remember, to deal
with divine things, to realize the grace
of the Gospel, to apprehend the peace
and healing of the cross, amid the
pain, and weariness, and weakness, of
their dissolving frame!

The ancient heathens erected no
altars to *death* amid their many altars
to their gods, known or unknown.
They knew the last enemy was inex-

orable. He would not be entreated. He would not be bribed. He would not spare. Make sure, then, O man, of the life beyond death, by believing in Him who is " Life eternal." So shall death be transformed from an enemy to a friend. It is said that one of old, seeing an artist painting death as a skeleton with a huge iron scythe, said, " Friend, should you not rather paint him as an angel with a golden key? " To the man who knows not the cross, and the forgiveness finished there, death must be the skeleton with the scythe. To the man who has found life and peace in believing the divine testimony to the great Sin-bearer and His work, death is the angel with the golden key. Which of these two is he to be to *you*, O fellow immortal? " He that overcometh shall not be hurt of the

second death." Is that your hope?
Is that a text which you expect to
place beneath your dying pillow? Or,
if you are to have no pillow but the
heaving wave, or, it may be, the red
turf of the battlefield, shall you be
able to take such a text to rest upon,
when called hence, perhaps in a moment, to receive the eternal judgment?

One old minister passed away with
these words upon his dying lips, " I
am full of the consolations of Christ."
Another Christian breathed out her
soul with, " Safe under the shadow
of His wing." Another spoke his in-
ward feeling in the hour of death with,
" Peace like a river." Melancthon was
asked, when dying, if he wanted anything. " Nothing but heaven," was
his reply. Baxter was asked when
about to depart, how he was, and answered, " Almost well." Grimshaw,

of Haworth, when asked the same question replied, "As happy as I can be on earth, and as sure of glory as if I were in it; I have nothing to do but to step from this bed into heaven." Dr. Judson said, "Death cannot take me by surprise, I feel so strong in Christ." Another Christian died with these words on her lips, "I never felt so near the Lord Jesus Christ as I do at this moment." Another once and again repeated the words, "Death hath no sting, Christ hath taken it away." Another exclaimed, "If this is the valley of the shadow of death, there is no darkness in it—it is all light."

"LET ME DIE THE DEATH OF THE RIGHTEOUS, AND LET MY LAST END BE LIKE HIS."

To him who reads these pages there may be but short time remain-

ing. " This year thou shalt die," were
the awful words that once came to
a sinner from a prophet's lips. And
though no prophet comes thus to
sound his trumpet in your ears, it
may not be the less true that this
year may be your last on earth.

Be it so or not, we speak to you
as one who still liveth upon this earth,
and to whom, therefore, in all its gracious plenty, the Gospel comes. It
speaks to you as a dying creature;
it speaks to your undying soul. It
speaks the words of grace; yet it urges
you to make haste. It points to the
open gate of the glorious city; yet
it says, that in a moment that gate
may be shut. It tells you of eternal
life through Him who died and rose
again. It assures you that whosoever
believeth is saved.

That which makes up the " good

news " for sinners, God has most fully
made known. We need not be at
a loss to find out what is " the gospel
of the grace of God." In love He
gave His Son, as the bearer of our
sins; as " the Lamb of God, which
taketh away the sin of the world."
In love He has written down for us
the whole story of the life and death
of this divine Sin-bearer. " The Word
was made flesh" at Bethlehem; the
Son of God there became very man,
bone of our bone, and flesh of our
flesh. There He who knew no sin
came under the burden of our sins.
For sin is so evil, and God is so just,
and the law is so holy, that either we
must bear our own sins or another
must bear them for us; they cannot
pass unpunished. There must be a
substitute, if there is to be salvation.
For thirty-three years " the Son of

the Blessed " dwelt among us, speaking
words of grace, doing deeds of mercy,
revealing God to us, carrying out the
great work of love, and completing
the great propitiation for sin.    He
went up to the cross as the Sin-bearer;
He went down to the grave as such;
He rose again the third day as one
who had done the whole work, and
who had been accepted by the Father
as such.    " He was delivered for our
offences, and rose again for our justi-
fication."    " He suffered, the Just for
the unjust, that He might bring us to
God."    " He hath made peace by the
blood of His cross."

All the perfection of Christ's person
and work is now presented to the
sinner, that he may receive it, and
be saved.    The Gospel comes to him
with the finished work of the Substitute, and presses that work on his

acceptance; so that in simply taking it as God presents it, he may stand on a new footing, even that of the perfectness of Christ, instead of his own imperfectness.

Thus we press the treasures of the Gospel on each reader of these lines. It speaks to you of the fulness of Christ, and the open way of access for you, a sinner, to all that fulness. It bids you welcome to the mercy-seat with all your worthlessness. It beckons you with the eager hand of love, to return to God and enter the city of refuge. It contains "good news" —the best of tidings to the sons of men; and it sums up with, " ONLY BELIEVE."

" THE AGES TO COME." Perhaps the eyes of some mourner may rest on these lines. Cast your sorrow upon Jesus, who is your Sorrow-bearer, as well as your Sin-bearer; and look forward to that city of light where darkness cannot dwell, neither sorrow nor crying; and where tears are wiped from every eye. The days of thy mourning shall be ended. The night shall pass away, and the morning star appear. Christian mourner, lean on the arm of your Lord, and pour your sorrows into His bosom. A lady, a missionary in Persia, was once teaching a class of inquiring natives. Worn out with the fatigues of a busy day, she could hardly sit erect. One of the converts, observing her weakness, placed herself behind her as a pillow, saying, " Lean on me." The loving teacher leant a little, but was afraid of leaning too much. The same kind voice again spoke out, " If you love me, lean hard." Oh, sorrowful Christian, lean on Jesus. He says to you, " If you love Me, lean hard."

"THE AGES TO COME." How soon
will they be here! With their untold
riches of joy, and song, and brightness,
they will soon be here. With their
happy re-unions, their everlasting fel-
lowships, their never-ending rest, their
never-setting suns, they will soon be
here! Our labors done, our victory
gained; our weariness at an end; our
vexations and troubles gone like a
dream of the night; our wounds all
healed; our heartaches soothed; our
heaviness of spirit exchanged for heavenly buoyancy; our ignorance all forgotten in divine wisdom and knowledge; our hanging hands lifted up,
and our feeble knees made strong;
our wrinkled foreheads smoothed by
the same tender hand that wipes all
tears from our eyes; all the imperfec-
tions of earth lost in the perfection of
heaven!

The arrival of all these things may be nearer than we think. For "He that shall come will come, and will not tarry." "What manner of persons," then, "ought we to be, in all holy conversation and godliness!" Surely we are called to a higher style of Christian life than most of us are living! How much holier, more prayerful, more unworldly. more self-denying, more loving and spiritual, ought all who name the name of Christ to be! We shall be like Him when we shall see Him as He is. Shall we not seek to be like Him here?

What makes us holy? Close intimacy with Jesus. What makes faith grow? Dealing much with Jesus. What fills us with joy? Looking into the face of Jesus. What keeps us steadfast? Leaning on the arm of Jesus. What comforts us in sorrow?

Resting on the bosom of Jesus. For
Christ *is* all and in all; and we have
all in Him. Let us seek to honor
His fulness by receiving it fully, and
to enjoy His love.